A PRACTICAL
COURSE IN

———— ⚡ ————

PERSONAL
MAGNETISM

'Doctor's Orders' brings together curious and curative treasures from the unique collections of Wellcome Library, London's world-famous medical library.

Wellcome Library is open to all readers looking to explore what it means to be human, where rare and unusual books on medicine, anthropology, psychology and belief systems sit alongside studies in alchemy, witchcraft, and more.

wellcome collection

WELLCOME COLLECTION is the free museum and library for the incurably curious. It explores the connections between medicine, life and art in the past, present and future. It is part of Wellcome, a global charitable foundation that exists to improve health for everyone by helping great ideas to thrive.

A PRACTICAL COURSE IN

PERSONAL MAGNETISM

The Victorian Guide to
Health, Happiness, Power and Success

Psychic Research Co.

P
PROFILE BOOKS

First published in Great Britain in 2017 by
PROFILE BOOKS LTD
3 Holford Yard
Bevin Way
London
WC1X 9HD
www.profilebooks.com

Published in association with Wellcome Collection

**wellcome
collection**

Wellcome Collection
183 Euston Road
London NW1 2BE
www.wellcomecollection.org

Body of text taken from *A Practical Course in Psychic Instruction:
Personal Magnetism*, by the Psychic Research Company (1891, 1901)

Inset material taken from *Concentration, and the Acquirement of
Personal Magnetism*, by O. Hashnu Hara (1906)

1 3 5 7 9 10 8 6 4 2

Printed and bound in Great Britain by
Clays, Bungay, Suffolk

A CIP catalogue record for this book is available from the British Library.

ISBN 978 1 78125 834 7
eISBN 978 1 78283 350 5

MIX
Paper from
responsible sources
FSC® C018072
FSC
www.fsc.org

Contents

* * *

Magnetising a glass of water.

INTRODUCTION

* * *

PERSONAL MAGNETISM IS THAT QUALITY IN MAN which attracts the interest, confidence, friendship and love of mankind.

The intention of the writer of this Course has been to convey in simplest form the secret of personal power to the understanding of the reader. He has tried to show how the reader may succeed in enjoying the fruits of his study here and at once; not when hopes have withered and powers of enjoyment have faded, and when knowledge is shorn of its usefulness, but now when such knowledge can be put to personal advantage.

The students of this Course say that the writer has succeeded. They say that the strict avoidance of theoretical discussions in this Instruction has helped them to grasp and apply the principle of Success, and that this Course satisfies where more pretentious, more ambiguous, more discursive theses have failed to please or instruct.

The writer, therefore, rests on the testimony of his students, making no apology for the intentionally personal and simple tone of the Instruction.

Preface by the Author

* * *

I SUPPOSE THE WISH THAT IS MOST COMMON TO MEN AND women is the wish to attract others, because this means power, influence, wealth, success, social prestige, popularity, satisfaction and love. It is a good wish; let that be made clear at the start. It is not debasing to aspire to influence. It is not a mean ambition to desire wealth; because wealth itself is but a means of increasing one's usefulness. Go back a score of years or more in your memory and you will recall that the great and influential men and women of the world were pointed out to you as examples worthy to be followed. They were shining lights in the eyes of those older than you. Your parents and teachers spoke of them with respect, and wished that you could follow in their footsteps and reach the heights they had attained. Were they in error in so exalting human character? I do not think so. The great minds of the world must ever be our beacons on our life-journey, and an analysis of the characters of the great ones living and dead yields us the secret of that philosophy of living which made their lives sublime, and full of power. Let me put before you the secret of their attainment.

In the first three lessons of this course I have endeavoured to enlighten you on some of the general characteristics of the study of Personal Magnetism and thus lead up to and prepare you for the specific instruction which follows.

LESSON I

THE STORAGE BATTERY ∞
THE PRESENCE OF MENTAL CURRENTS

THE STORAGE BATTERY

* * *

YOU PERHAPS HAVE NEVER THOUGHT THAT YOU ARE yourself a sort of electrical storage battery, constantly receiving and discharging force; sending out currents of attraction and repulsion continually, sometimes consciously, as when you desire to impress your friends, sometimes unconsciously, as when you make an agreeable or a disagreeable impression upon someone of whom you have taken no notice beyond a look. You are thus acting upon others and being acted upon by others with your will or against your will constantly and continually. That is your first Fact.

The Presence of
Mental Currents

* * *

Now there is a Force at work evidently.

Is it the Force of Thought?

No. Because it manifests itself without Thought on your part. It may be, and is, added to Thought.

Is it Electricity?

Electricity is only a name for an unknown Force.

What is it?

It is called Magnetism, because we do not know what else to call it. It may well be called a mental current, very like an electric current in many ways. It is a Force which we can learn to employ, learn to govern, as we have learned to govern Electricity without understanding its composition. It is a mystery in its source; let us simply accept it as we do the mystery of Life itself, and pass on to the use of the Force.

THE LAWS OF MAGNETISM

The first law of magnetism is that 'like magnetic poles repel one another, and unlike magnetic poles attract one another'. The human brain has also its positive and negative aspects, and its poles are situated respectively in the cerebrum and cerebellum. Figure I shows the ordinary magnetic lines radiating from an ordinary magnet, the space filled with the lines being the magnetic field.

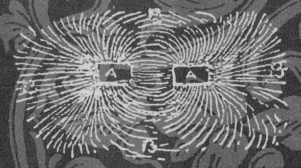

Figure I

Now coming to our immediate subject, Thought. You will readily understand how the thought field can follow the same lines as the magnetic field. Here is the brain and the thought field. Thus we get 'A', the brain, 'B', the thought lines of the thought field.

In the feeble, unorganised brain this field is weak, and affects only a limited area. But the greater the Personal Magnetism, the more powerful and organised the brain, the greater the extent of its radiation, the wider its field, the more lasting its effects.

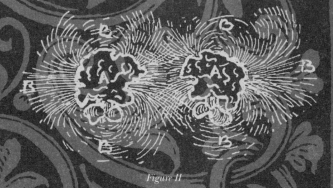

Figure II

Thus one person acts as a transmitter and the other as a receiver. The one is negative, the other positive. So like minds repel each other, and unlike minds attract, or perhaps it would be better to say that the strong mind attracts the weak, and vice versa.

But the great point is that one and all can take on this characteristic, and so increase their stock of magnetic and electric particles that they become vital!

The vital temperament radiates magnetism. The invisible currents pass off in every direction from every part of the body, and so great is the force of this subtle power that, although invisible to the naked eye, the camera can reveal it; and the human body and human mind at once feel the impression, bodily as a thrill, or sensation of warmth, mentally as an invigorating shock from an electric battery, or as an overpowering desire to 'go out and do something'.

Such a temperament has the ability to influence every person (and animal) who comes in contact with him. The acquirement of this life force applies to every grade of society and to both sexes.

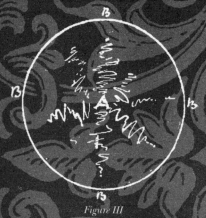

Figure III

Figure III clearly indicates the nature of thought sent in the general direction, but consisting of uneven and vacillating action, and will explain better than anything else why it is that some people have never achieved anything by the study of the many methods of improving 'thought life'.

LESSON II

CHARACTERISTICS OF THE MAGNETIC INDIVIDUAL ∽ A SENSE OF REST ∽ A PECULIAR GAZE ∽ ALWAYS POLITE ∽ THE WEAK GROW WEAKER AND THE STRONG, STRONGER ∽ THE MAGNETIC MAN PRESERVES KNOWLEDGE ∽ WORKS ACCORDING TO FIXED LAW ∽ NOT EAGER ∽ HE USES YOUR FORCE ∽ YOU LIKE HIM

CHARACTERISTICS OF THE MAGNETIC INDIVIDUAL

* * *

THE FIRST STEP SHOULD BE IN THE NATURE OF A critical observation of the operation of the force through people about us; noting differences in their characters and the logical effects of certain attributes.

We all know the type of the magnetic man or woman. Women are as magnetic as men, and if I use here men only as examples it is merely to avoid confusion in grammar; it is sufficient for the student to remember that everything which applies to man in this book applies equally to woman. In the attainment of Magnetism and influence the sexes are equal.

A Sense of Rest

* * *

WHEN YOU ARE IN THE COMPANY OF THE CONSCIOUSLY
Magnetic man, the first effect upon you is one of rest;
he is not nervous; he is not fidgety. Following the sense
of rest comes to you a recognition of a reserve strength
in him somewhere – you cannot place it; you cannot
localise it.

It is not exactly in his look; nor in his manner; nor
in his speech; nor in his actions; but it is there and it
seems to be a part of him.

That is the point exactly; it is a part of him, and a
few minutes previously, odd as it may seem to you,
it was in a small degree a part of you. A little of that
strength of attraction which he displays and of which
you are conscious went from you to him without your
knowledge.

But never mind that just now.

A Peculiar Gaze

* * *

LET US EXAMINE THE MAN A little more closely, that we may get at the secret of the fascination he exercises upon you. First, watch his look. His eyes hold you, but he is not staring at you. He is not looking into one or the other of your eyes; he is looking right between them at the root of your nose. His glance seems to go through you with an intent, boring gaze, but there is nothing offensive in it. You feel that he is not, and could not be, impertinent. Notice also that he does not look at you so when you are speaking; he waits, as it were, to receive your message, and then sends his to you. When he speaks he looks at you in that intent, masterful way, yet kindly. But he is not self-assertive; he is not argumentative.

A magnetic force often draws its force from others.

ALWAYS POLITE

* * *

HE LISTENS TO YOU WITH POLITENESS; HE IS POLITE
always, but you get the impression of an inflexible will
beneath that calm exterior; you sense power in him.
He is a man to be obeyed; in a word, the impression he
leaves upon you is that of one who knows exactly what
he wants and is in no hurry, because he is confident
that he will get it. Ah! now we have it in words. This
accounts for his calmness, his security. Knowledge is
power, and he knows that he rests his case upon the
laws of Cause and Effect.

The Weak Grow Weaker and the Strong, Stronger

* * *

It is the Law that the Positive must and shall act upon the Negative; that the Negative shall feel and admit the power of conscious strength; i. e., shall surrender something of magnetism to the strong. 'And from him that hath not, shall be taken away even that which he hath!' Do these words carry a new meaning to you now in the light of your present knowledge? Wonderful words. True in Law as well as true in sentiment.

The Magnetic Man
Preserves Knowledge

* * *

Now let us dissect his conversation. Does he impart any information to you? Very little, and nothing whatever that could be construed as at all self-assertive or vain; what he gives, is usually of no importance, though you seem to feel that it is, while you listen.

Works According to Fixed Laws

* * *

When this man brought to himself popularity, influence, wealth or success, he accepted them; took them as his right; as the logical sequence to the operation of the Law of Cause and Effect, and went on. He did not stand still. He brought Wealth to him in just the same way as he brought popularity to him, by Government. He governed by Magnetism; he attracted men; he wanted wealth; he attracted wealth because he wanted it.

WHY DRESS IS SO IMPORTANT

'FOR THE APPAREL OFT PROCLAIMS THE MAN.'
Shakespeare.
'WE ARE ALL CHARMED BY THE NEATNESS OF THE PERSON.'
Ovid.

'Neither virtue nor ability will make you appear like
a gentleman if your dress is slovenly and improper.'
The one who does not pay attention to his personal
appearance is making a fatal error. It is either his
recommendation or the reverse. The more prosperous
you look the more success you will attract. Let the
salesman or professional man wear out-of-date or shabby
clothes and he will find he will not do near as well as if he
was well dressed. He does not have confidence in himself.
His magnetism is not as strong because he does not feel
at his best. Clothes don't make the man, but they do help
him make an impression. When I speak so of clothes I do
not mean that you should try to be a Beau Brummell. To
spend money foolishly on dress is a mistake, but to spend
enough money so that you will look well is something
everyone should do.

Refinement, grace and charm are the weapons of
Personal Magnetism.

Not Eager

* * *

Now again, remember this adjective. He is not *eager*. He rather makes you feel that if he chose to do so he could say much. So he piques your curiosity a little. But he does not impress you as *purposely mystifying you*. Not at all. His eye is too frank for that, and if you know him for ten years you will find that he never lays conversational traps for you, to seek to extort your admiration. As a fact, his plane of thought is above admiration. In his early days, when he was learning, as you are learning now, how to acquire Personal Magnetism, he was perhaps pleased with the evidence of his power which the frank admiration of his acquaintances gave him, but he has outgrown that. Yet, he has outgrown it; no man ever stands still! There are always heights of endeavour beyond; we never reach the summit.

HE USES YOUR FORCE

* * *

NOW IF YOU GO BACK IN MIND TO YOUR CONVERSATION
you will find, though you did not notice it at the time,
that you were the one who told what you knew; you
were the one who sought to please; you were the one
who gave. Yes, that's it exactly; you gave; he received.
Had he willed it otherwise, he in his strength of
conscious knowledge, and you in your weakness and
unpreparedness; you would have been compelled to
receive from him whatever he chose to give of impulse,
of command, of opinion. Had he wished to do so, he
could have swayed you as the wind sways the rush in
the marsh. Why? Because it is the Law, and he knows
the Law while you do not. But he did not wish it at that
time; he merely permitted himself to make a pleasant
impression upon you; he did so, because he knew his
power, and taking a little magnetism from you, he left,
as the bee takes honey from the flower and goes his way.

You Like Him

* * *

But we are going too fast. This is a stage beyond our Lesson. What impression has this magnetic man left with you? Just this, that you wish to see more of him because you feel that he is in sympathetic touch with you in some mysterious way which you cannot define. You have 'taken' to him, and you do not get rid of his influence even after you have parted.

LESSON III

CHARACTERISTICS OF THE
NON-MAGNETIC INDIVIDUAL ∽
HE DEPRESSES ∽ HE IS A GRUMBLER ∽
THE REASON ∽ ADMITS FAILURE

CHARACTERISTICS OF THE
NON-MAGNETIC INDIVIDUAL

* * *

DO YOU KNOW THE NON-MAGNETIC MAN? THIS IS A GOOD place to put him on paper in contrast to the strong personality of whom we have just been speaking. He irritates you; if you are peevish yourself, he intensifies your irritation; if you are morbidly inclined, he deepens your gloom; if you are happy, he is something of a drag. Yes, he is a weight; you are called upon to lift him. He is asking for sympathy; he says he is misunderstood; he has a grievance against fate, against the weather, against some person.

HE DEPRESSES

* * *

YOU ARE GLAD WHEN HE IS GONE. HE HAS DRAWN upon you terribly because *you did not know how* to safeguard yourself against his influence. Had you known, you might have not only saved yourself a loss of magnetism but also drawn something even from his weakness if you had wished it.

HE IS A GRUMBLER

*   *   *

HE IS DISCONTENTED; HE IS A BABBLER; HE TELLS HIS secrets; he wants to share his troubles with you; he is the creature of impulse; without reserve; without calmness; without judgement; without poise; without attractiveness. Oh, flatter him and let him go. Get rid of him. You can reach him most easily through his love of self; pamper it and get rid of him – that is your thought; you put it at once into execution, and get him off your mind.

THE REASON

*   *   *

NOW WHAT IS THE REASON FOR HIS LACK OF attractiveness? It is as simple as A, B, C.

He is a dependent; a negative; he has grievances; grievances! Can you fancy the magnetic man of whom we have just spoken as a man with a grievance? Can you picture it? No, the thing is absurd. Your magnetic man is a power because he has subdued his circumstances, because he has held an attitude of mind which governs circumstances, which controls environment.

Admits Failure

* * *

Look at the other side of the picture. Here is your non-magnetic man a failure, by his own confession. Though he does not know it perhaps; weak complaining, inviting failure by his attitude of mind; a spendthrift of thought, a waster of energy; such a one is doomed to failure by the Law; the unalterable Law of Cause and Effect. Here are your two types. Study them well and carefully. The first is your model; the second your warning. As a golden rule to heed it may be dinned into your ears: *'Don't air your grievances. Seek not sympathy or flattery. Recognise the force in every desire and make that force your own.'*

THE VALUE OF CHEERFULNESS

The successful man is cheerful and hopeful. He has a
smile on his face, and meets everything that comes in
the same way. The cheerful man is creating new power,
while the pessimist is destroying his power. There is
nothing that will help you meet the hard turns in the
road, sweeten life and take out drudgery, like a sunny,
optimistic disposition. Two may have practically the
same ability, but if one is a cheerful thinker while the
other is despondent, and gloomy, the former will leave
him far behind. Cheerfulness is a tonic to the mind.
It dispels friction, worries, anxieties, and it will often
turn disagreeable experiences into agreeable ones. You
can do your best work only when you are in a cheerful
state of mind. When you are out of temper your entire
physical machinery is out of working order.

It should be your plan to follow the following
philosophy: try as much as you can to let nothing
distress you, and to take everything that happens as
for the best. Believe that this is your duty and that
you err in not so doing. The next time you are out
walking make it a point to look at every one you can.
See how many you see that look as though they are

happy. Notice the ugly grouchy expression on most people. You can make life one continuous round of sadness, instead of joy and gladness. How few there are who bring more sunshine into our lives, who scatter gladness and cheerfulness wherever they go. It is so seldom that we see one of these cheerful faces that everyone is attracted by it. Get the habit of looking pleasant, of radiating cheer, wherever you go. This will make you happier than to own many houses or any kind of possessions. It is free to you. All you have to do is to develop it. Your ability to radiate sunshine will add greatly to your power. It is not really hard to transform a gloomy disposition into a cheerful one. True, a cheerful face is but the reflection of a big glorious heart. You cannot look a part unless you feel it.

LESSON IV

GOING INTO SPECIFIC INSTRUCTIONS

* * *

HOW DID YOUR MODEL BECOME MAGNETIC? WHAT did he do with himself, and how was the effect produced? Natural questions these. Let me answer them as simply as I may. But let us drop the example and apply the instruction directly to you as an individual, that it may make a deeper impression upon you.

THE NATURE OF MENTAL CURRENTS

* * *

DESIRE, IN ANY FORM, IS A MENTAL CURRENT LADEN with power – just the kind of power which the magnetic man has over his fellows. When I say 'mental current' I speak literally. I am not merely using a figure of speech. All desires work on the plan of electric currents and are governed by similar, if not the same, laws of attraction and repulsion.

Extracting Power from Desire

* * *

WHEN YOU REALISE THAT FROM ANY FORM
of desire you can extract its power, magnetism, you
have, as it were, discovered a gold mine in your own
garden. For desire is ever at hand. It manifests its
source in many ways. You waste the force and thus
weaken your power of attraction when you give way
to desire. You discharge magnetism which you should
store up in order to attract the good things of life.

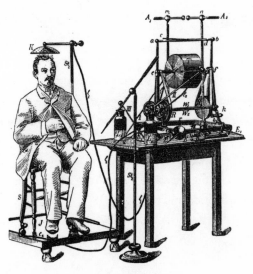

The Thought Machine.

PLENTY OF FORCE ON EVERY HAND

* * *

WHEN YOU LEARN TO LOOK UPON DESIRE, NOT AS a stumbling block, but as a stepping stone, your success in life is assured. The force of desire is manifested by many varieties of mental currents such as impatience, anger, dissipation, indulgence or vanity.

THE METHOD OF OPERATION

* * *

THE PLAN OF PROCEDURE NOW, THEN, IS UPON FEELING
a desire current to hold it within you – to refuse to gratify
it. By this conscious effort of your will you insulate
yourself against weakening discharge of force, and at
the same time create a condition of attractiveness which
will remain so long as that desire is not neutralised by
being gratified. Let us first take up a very common but
extremely weakening form of vanity current – the desire
to surprise.

DON'T BE A DOUBTER

To the doubter everything seems impossible, because

'OUR DOUBTS ARE TRAITORS,
AND MAKE US LOSE THE
GOOD WE OFT MIGHT WIN,
BY FEARING TO ATTEMPT.'
Shakespeare.

Nothing is impossible to a willing mind. If you want to succeed in anything you must have confidence in your own powers. That is the secret of those who rise. Your mind is made up of the material you gave it to digest. If you feed it on doubt, you are bound to have a doubting mind. From doubting something you gradually get to doubting everything you do. This kills success and self-reliance. From today on forget the two words 'doubt' and 'fear'. There is nothing you will ever be called on to do that you have not the power within you to do. The medical professors say that the human body is never given more pain than it can stand. If the suffering is beyond human endurance the person loses his consciousness. This is the same with the mind.

It is not asked to do something that it is not capable of accomplishing. We told you above if you give the mind doubt to digest, it will be a doubting mind. It works the other way. If you give it hope, it will be a hopeful mind. Doubt has no more place in your mind than poison in your mouth. Cast it out instantly if it tries to enter. Never say or think 'I can't do this' or 'Can I do this?' but always 'I can do this – I will do it.' You will find this kind of spirit will make you succeed. The person with a strong mind is able to concentrate on his work with such enthusiasm and power that he will conquer all difficulty. Positiveness creates confidence. You take up difficult problems and succeed, where a doubting person would not attempt them. Success makes the mind grow. The more you undertake and accomplish the more your mind expands. If you do not believe you can accomplish your object, you do not have that pointed attack and your effort is aimless. You would not become one of the leaders, but one that is led. As long as you have to be led you have not a free will. Assert your free will and you can become a leader and director of your destiny.

SECRECY IS YOUR INSULATION

* * *

FIRST, UNDERSTAND THE VALUE OF SECRECY. WHEN you come into possession of a piece of information, no matter how trivial, which it would please you to impart to an acquaintance, *keep silent*, because this is your first attempt to practise the *evolution of magnetism from repressed desire*. This secret of yours is a *unit of mental magnetism* stored up in your brain battery, and this secret held begets a force which draws more force to it from without just as your money in a bank draws interest. The more secrets you store up in your mind, the greater repression or insulation you are exercising; so the greater your command over your impulses; so the greater the store of your reserve-force, unwasted, unspent; ready to be of service to you in important enterprises.

RESTRAINT DOES NOT
MEAN DULLNESS

*   *   *

NEVER FANCY FOR A MOMENT THAT THIS HABIT OF repressing impulse will bring about a condition of dullness in which desire will be obliterated. The effect is the reverse; the desires become of tenfold strength and force, as a dammed-up river increases its pressure upon the banks – and then, when you are ready to use the power, it amounts to something. It has become a Force indeed.

EVIDENCE OF STRENGTH
IN DESIRE-FORCE

*   *   *

YOU HAVE NEVER ANALYSED THE FORCE OF A DESIRE perhaps. Think a minute. The desire to convey a piece of news to a friend may force you to jump into a cab and rush headlong into his presence. That must be a strong force in operation which can drive you to this activity. Well, the point is that you want that force yourself. Keep it. You need it if you are to attract to yourself the satisfaction and success you crave.

MYSTERY

* * *

THE NEXT POINT IS THAT THE WORLD YIELDS AUTHORITY to those whom it cannot understand. The deep river is silent. Who shall penetrate the depths of thought of the magnetic man? He is a mystery; you cannot gauge him because he will not permit it. He is unfathomable. You too must be a mystery; you must not be vulgar or advertise yourself in any way. To be in any way bizarre in conduct is fatal to true power. It is not the eccentricity of genius which attracts us. We revere the genius *in spite of* the eccentricity. Be careful, you my student, that you do not confuse the interest of idle curiosity which likes to be amused with the respect which we feel for that which is beyond our comprehension. Therefore *leave your acquaintance in the dark* concerning your attributes and opinions as far as is possible. Pique their interest in this manner, for example: your friend comes to you with an important piece of information. In the old days you would have expressed the liveliest surprise. You will change that. You will now receive the news kindly but calmly, almost without comment, and the effect upon your friend will be of astonishment that what has so deeply affected him has made so little impression upon you. You must

*In trying situations great men often hold their
supporters about them by the subtle power of mystery.*

show him that you are not uninterested, but he learns
from your reception of the news that you are less easily
thrown off your mental balance than he. Perhaps
he had not noticed it before. What is the result? He
recognises in you a poise of character, which he had not
given you credit for. It makes him curious. Ah, you are
beginning to gain his respect. You are a mystery to him.

HOW TO MAKE YOURSELF A GREAT POWER IN THE WORLD

You have in you that same divine, creative spirit that was in all our greatest men. The only difference between you and them is the difference in your mind power. You can develop this and be raised above your fellows, above your present superiors, above the disadvantages of your environment. The great spur that makes a man want to do things comes from within. You must train your mental forces all the time, until you awaken that wonderful power within you and put it to practical use. Mind is the creator of all that is made by man's hands. The greatness of your brain determines whether your work will be superior or inferior.

Say to yourself, 'I hold within my mind, in an equal or lesser degree, similar powers to those that Shakespeare had. I can raise myself above my fellows, out of the ruck of mediocrity, above worries and disappointments, by developing my mind. I can succeed in anything I plan, and I can plan noble deeds if my mind is big enough and broad enough. A little thought and care every day, a little trouble, a habit of thinking systematically and logically will, bit by bit, strengthen my mental faculties and reveal undreamed-of possibilities to me. "I am the master of my fate." I will develop this divine gift of mine. I will cultivate this divine soul, and I will make the deserts of my life blossom like the rose.'

The greatest work is done by conscientious attention to the smallest details and requires a great amount of labour in seemingly trivial matters. Success sometimes comes so slowly that you may think it not worth the effort. When you get to thinking this way, remember all men have thought the same. Whatever you wish to become keep it before you. Make your motto: 'My mental training will enlarge my brain powers and enable me to do great things.' Whenever you are pursuing knowledge you are not wasting your time. The more you know the better you are qualified to cope with the unexpected. The more information you have, the more responsibility you have of creating new ideas. The more you train your mind the more you will be able to make use of the information you have stored away. You should form the habit of looking ahead; of planning what you want to accomplish. You may think this all nonsense, but it works out, and all you want is results. The calling forth of this determination and perseverance will greatly strengthen your character and will do a good deal to make you a greater man. You should read the lives of Napoleon and Cromwell and see how hard they worked when they were so near failure, how they achieved victory through the force of their mental powers. Reading the lives of victorious men will give you the encouragement to persevere in developing yourself. Such books inspire you with noble thoughts and lofty ideas. They awaken in you the desire to do things and helps you to raise yourself above the mediocre people around you.

EFFECTIVE USE OF
MYSTERY BY GREAT MEN

* * *

THE GREAT LEADERS OF MEN IN HISTORY, WHEN IN SORE straits and in danger of losing their supporters, have often held their doubting henchmen together, and drawn united action and loyal support from the malcontents, by the charm of personal mystery. No doubt many of you remember Charles Stuart Parnell, the Irish leader in the English House of Commons, the 'uncrowned King' as they called him in secret. He occurs to me as a more appropriate example of the penetrating force of Personal Magnetism than even Napoleon, Wellington or Gladstone. In America, James G. Blaine more nearly approached him in personal sway over the hearts and intellects of his followers than any man of his generation. To his closest friends, Parnell was ever a mystery. Even Gladstone, his oft-time opponent, admitted his charm, his force, his simple directness of command. Parnell spoke very little – always to the point. His voice was never harsh or loud. If ever one man governed by the influence of secrecy and silence it was this man, holding in one hand the reins which guided the most rebellious and discontented faction ever gathered in a parliament. We are not concerned with the circumstances of his fall. He rose by intelligent self-confidence; by the exercise of the repressive influence, the force of Personal Magnetism.

USE FORCE FROM THE OTHER MAN

* * *

A FURTHER POINT FOR YOU TO REMEMBER HERE
is that silence does not mean unsociableness; by no
means; it is only the right word in the right place; the
habit of withholding; the habit of steadfast thought.
Draw out the other man. Remember here that as long
as you are a mystery to your acquaintances, you are a
power. Should you gratify their curiosity, to return again
to the electrical discharge simile, you have permitted
an exchange of currents, a satisfaction which means,
electrically, neutralisation. You have both given and
received, and the condition of attraction has ceased
for the time. But by preserving always the mystery, by
refraining from gratifying the curiosity, you are yourself
the attraction; you the magnet; they the steel.

A Caution

* * *

A CAUTION IS NECESSARY HERE FOR THE OVER enthusiastic and heedless student. Do not forget that you *must*, especially at the start, use great discretion, judgement and tact in all your experiments. It would be almost fatal to your success if the purpose of your changed demeanour were discovered. Do not let it be at all apparent that you desire to obtain and hold information which would satisfy either active or latent curiosity. Never openly seek to arouse curiosity. I suppose it is needless to tell any student never to talk about his studies, aims and desires in this line, for that would put your listener ever on his guard. In talking thus of yourself you are violating the first rule of the study of Personal Magnetism – that of *conserving personal information* – and gratifying vanity.

SEEK ALWAYS TO AVOID FLATTERY

* * *

THE ATTRACTIVE OR MAGNETIC MAN NEVER TALKS
of himself. The result is that he is more talked about,
admired and approved than if he devoted all his
cleverness to arranging little conversational coups
intended to flatter his vanity.

The student may say: 'This does not apply to me. I never
seek flattery.' Then you are the one in a thousand. All
people seek approbation in some form, to a greater or
lesser degree. Those who seek it most eagerly get the
least, because they do not retain and conserve the force
which attracts that form of mental current.

Lesson V

The Tremendous Force of Desire
for Approbation: How to Conserve
and Apply It ∽ Guard Against This
Leakage ∽ You Will Soon Notice
a Great Change

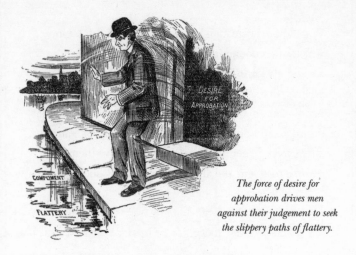

The force of desire for approbation drives men against their judgement to seek the slippery paths of flattery.

THE TREMENDOUS FORCE OF DESIRE FOR APPROBATION: HOW TO CONSERVE AND APPLY IT

* * *

EVERYONE CAN LOOK BACK ON HIS WEAKER MOMENTS and recognise the desire to tell something which he felt would directly or indirectly impress people with his importance, cleverness or uniqueness. This is the desire for approbation. It is a dominant force in human nature and is even noticed in animal life. It is nothing to be particularly ashamed of because it is natural. Its importance to us lies in the fact that it is a strong force which we have allowed to work against us.

When the average man has a chance to tell something which will redound to his credit, is he not almost *irresistibly impelled* to tell it? Does he not impatiently seek the first opportunity to tell it? Ninety-nine people out of a hundred are like that. They don't realise that that desire for approbation is one of the strongest of Nature's subtle *forces*. They don't realise that it *drives* them often *against their will* and always against their sober thought, better judgement and good taste. Above all, they do not realise that this subtle but almost irresistible force is a '*mental current*' that could be used for their own immense advantage instead of allowing it to 'discharge' flashily like the electric spark from the static machine, leaving them so much weaker than before.

Guard Against This Leakage

* * *

Student, take heed of this: check your desire for approbation at every turn. Let it not be satisfied even in the smallest thing. If it is hard to do this, that only proves that you are holding a strong force within you. A force which yearns and struggles to unite with its opposite outside in some other mentality. If that condition is held, then you have a state of attraction.

YOU WILL SOON
NOTICE A GREAT CHANGE

* * *

IT WILL NOT BE LONG AFTER YOU BEGIN TO PUT INTO
practice these ideas already given that you will notice
a marked change in yourself. A growing self-respect,
an unconscious dignity, a feeling of power. After each
conscious repression of desire-force you can *actually
feel* the power in your very nerves. Next you will notice a
difference in the attitude of others towards you, a greater
desire on their part to seek you out, to talk to and to be
with you. You can always hold and increase this condition
by remembering the rule of 'unsatisfied curiosity':

*Keep your friends wondering, but do not let them know
that you do so intentionally.*

HOW TO USE YOUR PERSONALITY TO WIN THE AFFECTION OF THE OPPOSITE SEX

Man draws much of his magnetism from woman. It is through her influence that he becomes refined and interesting. Many coarse, stupid and uninteresting men have changed themselves in a short time after having become interested in some woman. A woman of strong magnetism can accomplish wonders with a man in a short time.

There are, of course, numerous ways of gaining the admiration of those you wish to impress, but I will give only the most practical ones. First we should study the character of the one we wish to win. Love is first started into flame by sympathy – or by liking or pretending to like the things the other one likes. But right here let me warn you – never pretend. Oft-times to be sure, affection has been won by pretending to be in complete sympathy with the one desired, only to prove disastrous later on. Pretensions may do during a short courtship, but they will not make good after marriage. This is the cause of much of the unhappiness in married life. In true love there is no pretence. There is entire sympathy with each other's aims and ideals. It is not meant that both should be the same in character; neither is it expected that their wishes shall be identical in all respects; but there must be a general inclination towards the same desires and tastes.

Love and Courtship

The development of your powers of fascination and how to use them to the best advantage is a study in itself. Mere attraction between male and female is not real love, although it may develop into love by the great law. There are very few men and women who know anything of the real qualities they should possess. They do not know how to select one of the opposite sex worthy of real love. But anyone who reads this work cannot give this lack of knowledge as an excuse hereafter. Real love makes a wonderful change in a person. A couple meet and in time they become very much fascinated with each other. The man obtains power over the girl. She is willing to leave what has been the dearest things in her life – her home and family – for the man she loves. She will sacrifice everything for him. The same is true of the man.

Far more may be accomplished with gentleness than with brute force. There is a certain knack of doing things that brings results. The person who uses tact may get his own way about things and yet make it appear that it is the other one who is leading. Headstrong persons have to be managed in this way.

Marriage is one of the most important steps in life which a man or a woman can take. It can be the blessing of both, or it can be the ruination of both. It is a deplorable fact that observation reveals more unhappy marriages than happy ones. There must be a cause for this, and there is. The fault lies in the fact that couples marry when they are not suited to each other. If they would be more careful in their selections and, instead of marrying too early in life, take time to improve themselves, as suggested in this work, there would be more happy marriages.

Nature's plan was no doubt that everyone should marry. The majority of persons want to marry, but there are thousands and hundreds of thousands who do not marry, and as a result live a lonely and miserable existence. There must be a cause for this and it may generally be found in the fact that so many lack the power of attraction, or Personal Magnetism. You will never find the magnetic person devoid of plenty of opportunities to marry. They are able to fascinate and control the minds of others.

How to Cultivate Magnetic Beauty

There are people who are considered very homely yet they have so much magnetic beauty that they are great favourites. It is an absolute fact that a girl with a very homely face, and who has an ugly expression, can, if she is honest at heart, transform herself so she will seem beautiful to everyone who knows her, if she will form the habit of holding in her mind the thought of beauty. Not the superficial thought of physical beauty only, but the deep heart and soul thought of beauty. The kind of beauty that far surpasses any other sort of beauty is a kindly, helpful heart, and a wish to brighten the lives of others; to scatter sunshine here and there; and good cheer. When this is done it brightens the face and makes it beautiful. A beautiful character cannot help affecting and making a beautiful life.

We express outwardly what we express inwardly; our emotions, manners and bearing depend on our thoughts. If these are as they should be, you cannot help becoming sweet and attractive. The most prized beauty is within the reach of everyone.

LESSON VI

HOW TO USE ANTAGONISTIC FORCES FOR
YOUR OWN BENEFIT ∞ RECOGNISING
THE AVAILABLE FORCE ∞ A SPLENDID
EXERCISE FOR ABSORBING ENERGY ∞
YOU RISE ABOVE TEMPTATION

How to Use Antagonistic
Forces for Your Own Benefit

* * *

IN THE FOREGOING LESSONS IT IS SHOWN THAT
impulse or desire is a force – the very kind of force you
would like to exert in influencing others. You must
clearly understand now, if you do not already, that
every desire is a mental magnetic force, either Positive
or Negative; that it seeks to unite with its opposite –
to be satisfied just as the positive pole of the magnet
attracts the negative pole of the steel. To the student
who doubts the strength of these forces, let me point
out the case of the drunkard. What can drive a man
against his will and every instinct of his moral self –
save a tremendous though subtle force? In this instance
the force is temptation – a strong form of desire. I will
tell you how you can trick this vicious force so that, like
the Japanese wrestlers, you can use the strength of your
opponent against himself.

The magnetic man welcomes forces that
others dread, because he can extract a
precious power therefrom.

RECOGNISING THE
AVAILABLE FORCE

* * *

YOU HAVE LEARNED TO RECOGNISE THE MAGNETIC
value of secrecy and the suppression of vanity. Now
I want to impress upon you that all temptation is a
blessing in disguise. The intelligent student of Personal
Magnetism will welcome temptation in any form
because he has learned that to 'bottle up' its wanton
force within himself is to add to his mental magnetic
storage battery or Personal Magnetism. It adds to
his power of attraction. But to yield to temptation,
to satisfy the desire, to 'shoot the spark', as it were,
neutralises the attractive condition and weakens the
battery. The safeguard, the insulation of your mental
battery, is knowledge, the particular kind of knowledge
you are deriving from these lessons.

A Splendid Exercise
for Absorbing Energy

* * *

I will now give explicit information regarding the *method of conserving energy*. Suppose you feel yourself attacked by a desire or temptation of some kind. Ordinarily it would annoy you, to say the least. But now you recognise and welcome it, as just so much new force for your battery – so much capital.

Now concentrate your mind on this desire – get the benefit of its *full force* and then begin very slowly to inhale a long full breath to the extreme capacity of your lungs.

This should occupy about eight seconds. As you draw in this breath, repeat mentally to yourself: '*I now consciously appropriate the full force of this desire.*'

Then hold the full breath for the period of about eight seconds and repeat mentally: '*I now consciously absorb this force and it is henceforth my own property.*'

Lastly, exhale the breath for eight seconds, slowly and evenly, repeating mentally: '*I now have perfect balance and poise with which to control the magnetic force I have been storing.*'

This may be repeated several times if desirable.

I give this breathing exercise not only as a suggestion to fix the idea of appropriation, absorption and poise, but also because it is now generally believed among mental scientists that there is a very close relation between the lungs and the emotional nature of man.

You Rise Above Temptation

* * *

I WISH TO IMPRESS THE POINT RIGHT HERE THAT temptation loses its power over you the moment you realise that you can trick it; rob it of its force and use that force for your own ends. Thus, at a step, *you are placed above temptation* – a position men struggle all their lives to reach.

To make the point still more clear, let us compare temptation to a bombshell. It falls near you with lighted fuse. Knowing its nature and construction, you act quickly and intelligently. You pluck out the fuse. Then the power of the bomb is yours to use as you see fit. The ignorant man would have allowed the explosion to take place and suffered the results.

LESSON VII

The Time Required for Appreciable
Results ⟋ Some Effects Noticeable
at Once ⟋ As an Instance ⟋
What You Should Do

THE TIME REQUIRED FOR APPRECIABLE RESULTS

* * *

SOME STUDENT MAY SAY THAT THE FOREGOING
lessons are too simple; that he wants something more
mysterious and complex. To him I merely say: 'Follow
instructions and see for yourself. You can learn in no
other way.' He would be unreasonable indeed who
would expect a radical change in his character to be
brought about immediately on practising any exercise
given herein. These lessons show you the law governing
this subject and thus give you the chance to grow
without hindrance. Give the sunlight a chance at the
plant and the plant will thrive. It does not jump at once
into full bloom – it must have time to develop naturally.
In the case of the student, the light is let in to him
through the explanation of the law, and so surely as he
takes *advantage of the law*, so surely will he grow.

The non-magnetic man wastes his power
through ignorance of the laws of attraction.

SOME EFFECTS
NOTICEABLE AT ONCE

* * *

USUALLY THE NEW STUDENT NOTICES THE EFFECTS OF his development in about four or five days. A sensation which comes almost *immediately*, however, is one of increased self-respect and self-confidence. After each conscious retention of the force of a desire, an actual physical sensation of power and fullness is noticed in the brain and nerves. This is not at all like conceit or vanity. It is not assertive in the least but simply restful and reassuring. Let the beginner criticise himself frankly. Do not make the mistake of laying the blame for your lack of attraction upon the selfishness or bad taste of others. Whatever the fault has been, be sure it was all yours.

As an Instance

*   *   *

WATCH YOURSELF CLOSELY AS YOU MEET YOUR FRIENDS today. There is Mr B. now. For some reason you have always wanted his admiration and close friendship. You feel that he does not take an interest in you; that your company does not satisfy him. Examine your past conduct towards him for the reason. You find that *he* has been the receiving battery while you have been the one to 'shoot your spark' to him, weakening yourself each time in your effort to satisfy your conscious or unconscious desire for approbation.

Do you get it? No. Does he get yours? Yes. Does he endeavour to get it? No. Perhaps you can now refer more intelligently to the principles of conserving forces explained in the foregoing lessons. Mr B. is drawing force from you instead of you drawing it from him.

WHAT YOU SHOULD DO

*　*　*

STOP. YOU ARE ON THE WRONG TACK. PONDER ON THE philosophy of the principles already set forth. Let Mr B. alone for a few days. Practise intelligently the conservation of these forces which you have been throwing away. Have you done anything today that it would flatter you to relate? *Keep it to yourself.* Bottle it up resolutely. It seems easy, but your habit of letting these little sparks fly for the momentary satisfaction it gives has grown strong upon you. Time and again you will find them escaping your vigil and each time leaving you flat, foolish and non-magnetic. Conserve the desires of the flesh as well as the desires of the mind. This is not merely the old doctrine of self-denial. It is the scientific law of the force, mental currents. It is *not* difficult to follow because with an intelligent understanding of the law you can now see that you are doing far more than merely resisting a force. You are making that force your own. *You capture it*, and can use it as you see fit.

LESSON VIII

THE STUDY OF EFFECTS ⤬
A PHYSICAL CHANGE NOTED ⤬
A PECULIAR RESULT

THE STUDY OF EFFECTS

* * *

SOME STUDENTS MAY HERE AS: 'SUPPOSE I DO capture all these forces, catching the force within each mental and physical desire as it comes, and storing all this energy, what effect will this have?'

The energy you have thus stored attracts its opposite from other people as surely as positive electricity attracts negative, and even without conscious effort on your part. Your face, your manner and your actions will unconsciously change. You will find the good things you formerly sought in vain *drifting towards you* unsought. They are bound to come. It is the law of attraction. When good things are coming your way don't be too impatient. Don't grumble if 'the particular good thing' you have been wanting doesn't jump at you. It will come.

A Physical Change Noted

* * *

WHEN A MAN BEGINS TO DEVELOP HIS MAGNETIC personality on the lines suggested, his body actually undergoes a physical change. His eye is brighter, his skin clearer, his carriage more erect and the expression of lurking fear, of worry, of embarrassment, of depression, leaves his face. He is no longer the unfortunate *object* of the subtle forces of human nature. He is a conscious *force* himself. The world, so far as he is interested in it, appears to him in a new light. He slowly begins to realise his power and because he himself knows and understands this thing he is satisfied.

A PECULIAR RESULT

* * *

WHEN THE STUDENT HAS REACHED THIS STAGE HE should ever be on his guard against the danger of leakages. To even speak of this precious consciousness of power would be to lose much of it. A peculiar phenomenon I may mention and one which only the shallowest thinker will consider a discouragement is the fact that as you acquire this power, and 'fortune' seems at last to have turned in your favour, the things which you have sought in vain and which now are drifting towards you *have lost some of their value in your eyes*. This does not make the true student unhappy. Quite the reverse. He glories and finds satisfaction in his *sense of power*. Remember there are other desires greater than those you now entertain.

LESSON IX

HELPFUL SUGGESTIONS FOR
PRACTICAL APPLICATION ∽
THE CENTRAL GAZE ∽ HOW TO GAIN
EASE AND SELF-CONFIDENCE ∽
THE MAGNETIC HANDSHAKE

HELPFUL SUGGESTIONS FOR PRACTICAL APPLICATION

* * *

AFTER THE STUDENT HAS THOROUGHLY FIXED in his mind the theory of conservation of the force within mental currents and the resulting state of attraction, it may be well for him to remember a few novel but effective suggestions which will help him to put his new knowledge more quickly into effect.

Let us first take a case where it is desired to make a favourable impression under difficulties. Suppose you are about to have an interview with a man whose personality has always oppressed you. Let us say that he is one of the big, blustering, bold-eyed, bull-necked kind, a man of weight in his community, but entirely without the finer sensibilities, and as thick-skinned as he is cruel. For a refined, sensitive person it is misery to deal with such a man, especially if favour or concession is to be asked. Coarse natures love to

make the cringing ones cringe the more. But to our
point. You can deal with this type very handily. Your
previous knowledge and training in the conservation of
forces guards you from any attack he could otherwise
make upon your sensitiveness through your weakness
or vanity. You therefore appear before him in a true
and modest light, feeling with justice that you could
represent yourself far more favourably if you cared to.
This very knowledge is a force that will show in your
face in spite of yourself and will go far to impress or
repress the opposing force you are about to encounter.
With your consciousness of reserve force you quietly
and confidently begin your conversation. Let no sign
of eagerness, uneasiness or anything but pleasant, easy
quietness and unobtrusive self-assurance be apparent
in your manner.

The Central Gaze

* * *

WHEN YOU ARE TALKING LOOK HIM DIRECTLY *BETWEEN his eyes*. That is, at the root of his nose. Imagine that you are looking at a minute speck at that point and that you see the weak spot in this man's character (for all such coarse people are mean and weak, really) and then you must talk to that speck of a man *between his eyes* and *look calmly* as you do it. Don't glare or scowl. You will find him soon shifting his eyes uneasily. Make him look at you; make him keep his eyes on yours while you are talking. But when *he* talks, shift your gaze. Look at his waistcoat, his boots, anything but his eyes. Listen respectfully, and the instant you begin to speak again, seek out that speck between his eyes. Do none of these things conspicuously. Do not let him get an idea that you are testing anything on him. Calmness is your keynote.

That man will remember you. Whatever the result of your interview you may rest assured that he will remember you; that you have done the best that could be done; that you have made more of an impression on him than he likes to admit even to himself.

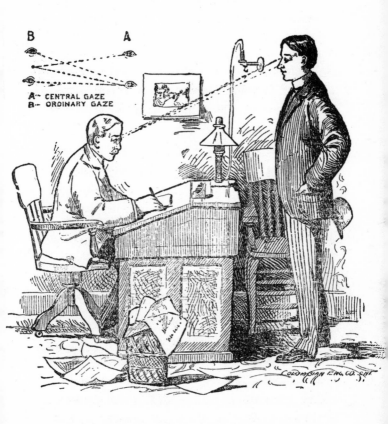

*A hard interview made easy by a knowledge
of the laws of mental currents.*

How to Gain Ease
and Self-confidence

* * *

AN EXERCISE WHICH WILL GIVE YOU GREAT EASE
of manner, pleasing address and confidence in yourself
is that of practising alone upon imaginary people. You
should be absolutely alone where none can see or hear
you. An open field is the best place, but locked securely
in your room you will be comparatively safe from
observation.

Spend five minutes first in taking very slow and deep
breaths – inhaling to the full capacity of your lungs and
exhaling very slowly and evenly. Then get up smartly
on your feet and address an imaginary person of your
acquaintance. You may use your own image in a mirror
or depend entirely on your imagination for a figure. You
can, of course, say anything you like, no matter how
extraordinary, but you must think out each sentence
beforehand. Then address the image in strong, full,
confident tones. Round out each syllable and dwell upon
it. Let your words ring out – straight from the chest.
Point your finger, pace the floor, use impressive gestures,
do and say anything you would like to do and say were
the person addressed actually present.

An interesting and beneficial interview with a 'live ghost'.

This is a splendid exercise. It will develop self-confidence in anybody and its effects will be noticed in many indirect ways, which I have not the space here to mention, but which you will recognise at once.

A half-hour of this unique work whenever you feel depressed or need stimulation of your self-confidence will produce wonderful results. The student is also often helped towards definite material results by thus using the power of auto-suggestion, through the forcefully spoken word. *Ask for what you want – demand it as if you owned it.*

MAGNETIC HANDS AND FINGERS

If you can gently slap a person on the shoulder in a more artful than a bold way, and at the same time concentrate your mind upon the contact and will that you emit a current of your magnetism to them you will find that in many cases he will experience a tingling feeling of warmth or a noticeable shock as from an electric battery.

There is no one that is not susceptible to magnetism, but there is a big difference in people. Those who have a powerful mentality could only be influenced by another of exceedingly powerful mentality. Before you can influence another they must be in a passive or open mind. Those who you think you could least affect would be the easiest for you to affect. Never try to influence a person when they are excited, nervous or under great anxiety or mental trouble. If these conditions exist try to remove them by sympathy, cheerfulness and your assurance that everything will probably turn out all right in the end. The more passive a person is, the easier he is to affect.

The hands can be made a powerful means of imparting your magnetic fluid to others. If your hands are naturally soft and silky, and perspire freely, it is of great help, as the magnetic fluid has an easy outlet. But if your hands are not so they must be made so by dabbing them with some good oil every night. Also rub your hands together a good deal. In this way your circulation is increased. This will soften and freshen them up, and cause the magnetic fluid to flow more freely. Whenever you have the chance of placing your hands on one you wish to influence you should do it, and at the same time will that you are imparting a flow of your magnetism to them. This will arouse the force within you and increase your magnetic power.

THE MAGNETIC HANDSHAKE

*   *   *

THE HANDSHAKE IS ALSO AN IMPORTANT MATTER IN meeting people. Looking him pleasantly between the eyes, grasp your friend's hand firmly, well up around the back and palm. Don't shake his fingers. After a quick, warm pressure draw your hand away, passing your fingers down his palm and off at his fingertips if possible. *It is the natural grip of cordiality and must have its effect.*

LESSON X

THE CULTIVATION OF THE
MAGNETIC GLANCE ∞ THE MIRROR
EXERCISE ∞ THE EFFECT

THE CULTIVATION OF THE MAGNETIC GLANCE

* * *

AFTER THE STUDENT HAS LEARNED AND DEMONSTRATED to himself the value of the conservation of mental currents, he really needs but little other help. Still, a few aids to development may seem important to some students and I will mention some.

In the preceding lesson, the method of gazing at a point between the eyes of the person addressed is described. For the sake of convenience we will refer to that method as 'the Central Gaze'. Do not make the mistake of using this promiscuously on any and all occasions. *It is solely for the purpose of making yourself impressive when you wish to be so. There is such a thing as being oppressively impressive, and this is to be avoided.* Use your force with tact and discretion. Pleasantness is attractive. Be pleasantly impressive. When you are trying to please, as in ordinary social intercourse, let your face wear an interested expression. Do not indulge in perpetual smiles, than which there is nothing more undignified, but practise and assume such an expression as comes to your face when you are witnessing a scene in which you are quietly interested.

Use the Central Gaze frequently, 'but back it up' with
a dignified pleasantness. You thus give a combined
impression of good humour and power.

THE MIRROR EXERCISE

*   *   *

HERE IS AN EXERCISE THAT WILL AID IN THE
development of an effective gaze and expression. Place
a small mirror on a table before you, or stand before a
large mirror with your face about fifteen inches from
the glass. With a pencil or some other dull-pointed
instrument, make a little dot or dent on the root of your
nose directly between the eyes. This mark will remain
about ten or fifteen minutes, and is for the purpose of
assisting to concentrate your attention and gaze. In
looking at your image in the mirror, focus your gaze
unfalteringly upon that spot between the eyes. Remain
perfectly motionless, gazing fixedly at the central point.
Try to keep from blinking. When you feel impelled to
blink, simply raise the lids a little instead; the relief to
the nerves is nearly the same as if you closed the lids.

This exercise should not be continued for longer than
fifteen minutes. Beginners may find it difficult to even

sit perfectly motionless for five minutes, but this repose
and nerve control should be learned if the student
wishes to develop fully.

Ready for an exercise. Cultivating a magnetic eye.

THE EFFECT

* * *

THE EARLY MORNING IS THE BEST TIME FOR THIS
exercise, when the brain is fresh and the body is rested and
nerves relaxed. Start in with a five-minute exercise and
gradually lengthen it each morning, one minute per day until
you can do the full twelve or fifteen minutes. After about
three days you will begin to notice the power and steadiness
in your gaze. You will note the weak shifting gaze of other
people. You will note that even those with a bold gaze look
into the one or other of *your eyes* and that they shift uneasily
when you calmly apply the Central Gaze, of which they are
of course unconscious. This Central Gaze strangely enough
gives you the effect of looking right through or into the
centre of the head of the person looked at. At the same time
it relieves you from the gaze or expression of his eye.

The mirror exercise just described rapidly develops a
powerful and magnetic eye. The eye is the window of the soul
and among psychic sensitives thoughts are often read from eye
to eye. You cannot be too careful to develop a masterful eye.
Should it happen that the student habitually wears glasses, the
effect of the exercise is still the same, but more care should be
used not to strain the eyes. *The fact that you wear glasses does
not materially weaken your ability to cultivate your gaze, and
indeed sometimes adds impressiveness.*

ACHIEVING BALANCE: SOME SECRETS OF INFLUENCING OTHERS

You may completely control the actions of others without their suspecting it. They may think all the time that they are doing just what they want to do, instead of which they are carrying out your wishes. A person may be so completely under the influence of another that his body is controlled by that other's thought. This is done when the hypnotist puts a subject to sleep. While under this influence the subject's mind is put out of use. The operator controls the body of his subject as if it were his own. The only way to make sure that you are not being controlled by another person is to form the habit of sitting alone and meditating before you decide any great problem. The habit that some men have of taking a proposition under advisement over night is a good one. You will find the answer you have arrived at by morning will be the best one for your guidance.

The question often arises: 'How is it that each year finds fewer and fewer powerful men are being developed?' Or why is it that there are not more magnetic men born? We cannot speak of the past, but I can speak of the present. I think that men of today as a general thing have more magnetism than ever before. This is the natural process of evolution. As man develops higher and higher in the scale of progression, he has more magnetism. But still you say that this does not answer your question, so I will explain more specifically. In the present age we have to go at such a pace that after a day's work our magnetic force is greatly diminished. Instead of retiring early and spending the night in quiet repose, giving nature a chance to restore this magnetism, more work is done at night. The business is carried home and the work for the next day is planned. If not business, then a round of exciting festivities is indulged in. The result is that instead of restoring the lost magnetism, more is expended. This is why people get old before they should. They do not give nature time to restore their forces. The person who does his work in the office and forgets it when he leaves his place of business will accomplish a great deal more in the long run, because he will be able to put more real energy into his work. The evenings should be spent in some phase of enjoyment very different from the work of the day. To do your best work you must enjoy yourself. Enjoyment means interest in life. Those who do not enjoy life do not really live, and lead an uninteresting life. When a man works until he is all tired out it takes him a longer time to recuperate.

Few of us realise how important a part in our life the mind takes. If you have worked hard all day and are tired from your efforts, and then spend the evening with others who are equally de-magnetised, talking of their work and expressing their worn-out feelings, you will feel worse than ever. But, on the other hand, no matter how tired you are, if you go home and take a bath and change your clothes, and spend the evening in company with others who have done likewise, you will find not only that you enjoy associating with them, but that your magnetism is restored. There is an exchange of magnetic force that is mutually helpful. Wives make a big mistake when they work all day and then show that they are tired out at night. They might have worked much less hard if they had but thought they could. Don't greet your husband with that tired expression. He is already tired, and when he takes on your mental condition his weariness is that much exaggerated. When a person is over-tired the least little thing makes him irritable and cross. Those of you who are married or going to be, think this over.

LESSON XI

THREE PRIVATE METHODS OF DIRECT
RADIATION OF THE MAGNETIC INFLUENCE

(1) MENTAL PHOTOGRAPHY

(2) THE SOLAR-PLEXUS METHOD

(3) THE MUSCULAR METHOD

THREE PRIVATE METHODS OF
DIRECT RADIATION OF THE
MAGNETIC INFLUENCE

* * *

IN EACH OF THESE THREE METHODS THE FIRST STEP
necessary is the 'retirement into silence.' This means
that the student is to retire to a quiet room, free from
disturbance, place himself in a comfortable position,
sitting or reclining, and give himself up wholly for
about ten minutes to absolute passivity, in both body
and mind. Every muscle should be relaxed and every
disturbing thought banished. When the student feels
that he has accomplished this, he is ready to take up
any of the three methods of throwing his force out into
active service on his behalf. I will describe the three
methods.

(1) Mental Photography

After getting into the calm and passive state, sit at a table and write a terse suggestion very plainly on a white sheet of paper. For instance, write:

'I *will* that my troubles with John Jones cease,' or 'I *will* impress So-and-So favourably,' or 'I *will* that So-and-So be impelled to do this.' After writing your desire plainly and briefly, sit back comfortably and gaze fixedly at it, concentrating intensely, yet with calmness, on the meaning of the lines before you, breathing slowly and deeply meanwhile.

This is Mental Photography. The theory is that forceful mental currents are thus most perfectly formed. If you begin with reasonable and simple requests of a general nature, such as desire for a gradual improvement in Health, an improved and strengthened character, a better memory, a sweeter temper, you will probably succeed from the start, and as you develop you can make your demands more definite and go more into details as in the examples just mentioned. So long as you ask for things which do not in any way, directly or indirectly, *conflict with the rights or happiness of other people* you will meet with a degree of success based upon the sincerity and intelligence with which you adopt your instructions.

Mental Photography. Forming, absorbing and radiating a thought force.

(2) The Solar-Plexus Method

The solar plexus is the great nerve centre in the spinal cord situated behind the pit of the stomach. Some scientists claim, and with very good logic, that this is really a brain – the abdominal brain – and that it controls not only certain involuntary bodily functions, such as breathing and heart pulsations, but also the emotional nature of the individual. A few mental scientists now look upon the solar plexus as a veritable magnetic centre or nerve magnet capable of affecting, or being affected by, the personality of others. These scientists operate as follows.

After going into the silence and becoming properly passive they lie prone upon a couch, having first removed all clothing which binds or hampers the movements in any way. Taking in a deep breath, they expand the chest, drawing in the abdomen at the same time. Then, holding the breath, they collapse the chest, forcing the air into and thus distending the abdomen. Collapsing the abdomen will again fill the chest if the breath is still held.

Stimulating the solar plexus for the radiating-vibration theory.

With each breath the chest and abdomen are each collapsed and distended alternately five times rather rapidly. A rest of half a minute follows and the act is repeated. Another rest of half a minute and it is repeated for the third and last time.

The attentive student can readily see that this exercise acts directly upon the solar plexus, giving it a stimulating internal massage through the movement of adjacent organs. The mental side of the idea is that the desire to be gratified must be *held calmly in mind* during the exercise, and that the stimulation of the solar plexus or nerve battery sends out the thought in vibrations which take effect upon the more or less receptive nervous organism of the other persons who are concerned.

Much is claimed for the effectiveness of their system, but whatever its virtue in affecting others, it certainly has a remarkable effect upon the student so far as giving him poise, calmness and relief from depression are concerned.

(3) The Muscular Method

The third and last method may seem to you rather bold in theory. The theory is that all force, whether expressed as Intelligence, or Mind, Gravity, Electricity, Muscular action, etc., is the same in essence, differing only in forms of expression. On this theory the student, after going into the silence, stands erect and contracts every muscle in his body to a state of intense rigidity so far as he is able to do so. Here, then, certainly is force, generated but unused. But the mind of the student is fixed intently upon the desire to be gratified. He is powerfully *willing* its fulfilment. At the same time he assures himself that the physical force-expression (the rigidity of his muscles) is changing into a mental force-expression. He is holding the thought that as the force oozes from his tiring muscles it goes out from him in the mental form of his desire and in that form acts upon the personalities or conditions concerned. This has been tried upon general business conditions with marked success. Each morning for a week a friend of mine practised this exercise with the thought 'Business will improve' and the result was successful.

'Why didn't you keep on?' I asked.

'I don't know,' was the frank reply, and the student would probably render such a response himself. A wonderful truth, tried, proved and successful, is often neglected because its very simplicity induces a lack of faith.

HOW TO PROTECT YOURSELF AGAINST INJURIOUS THOUGHT ATTRACTION

Never expect something you do not wish to happen. Expectancy is a powerful magnet. By your desire you attract what you want. If you fear something and think about it, you attract it to you. The law works for and against you unless you know how to control the forces. If you are thinking about something that you don't want to happen, don't you see you are attracting this just the same as if you desired it? Many teachers tell you that you can do away with fear by repeating, 'I'm not afraid,' not realising that you are thus admitting that you are afraid. A better plan is to say: 'I am full of courage. I am able to protect myself. Why should I be not as strong as anyone else? Why should I think that someone can hurt me by his thoughts or action? I am positive, not negative.' If at any time you feel inclined to fear, say over and over again: 'I have courage – courage.' You cannot say this and think it and yet suffer from fear at the same time.

LESSON XII

FAITH ASSISTS, BUT NOT ESSENTIAL ∽
ACQUIRED FAITH: SUCCESS
THROUGH PSYCHICALLY
PROVOKED IDEAS ∽ IDEAS OFTEN
THE CONNECTING LINK

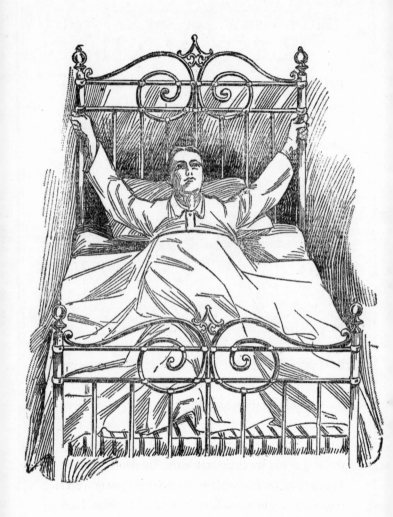

Faith Assists, but not Essential

* * *

EVEN IN THE FOREGOING EXERCISES IN PERSONAL
Magnetism, Faith, though not essential, adds much
to their effectiveness. I realise how hard it is for the
beginner to have faith in things he knows nothing
about and therefore take this occasion to give a word of
advice on the subject.

Acquired Faith: Success Through Psychically Provoked Ideas

* * *

YOU PROBABLY ADMIT THAT FAITH WOULD HELP YOU
along faster, but say you have no faith. Even without
Faith you can develop in Personal Magnetism, but with
Faith you can do better. Therefore, let me tell you that if
you really desire the advantage which Faith would give,
you can get it merely by *refusing to consider doubt*. That
is not so hard as it seems. The fact that you are studying
shows that you are anxious to learn. Therefore, you are
willing to follow instructions. It won't hurt you or weaken
you in any way to refuse to consider doubt at least. Look
upon that as part of your task, and remember that to

refuse (even temporarily) to consider doubt is practically the same as to have faith, and can be done by anyone who is sincere in his desire to learn. Many a student has been helped over rough places by adopting this 'negative' plan of acquiring faith and I have yet to find a sincere student who cannot operate it successfully. The intelligent Mental Scientist does not claim that the methods just described are alone in themselves wholly sufficient to bring about satisfactory results. Faith without work avails nothing, and work without faith is about as useless.

IDEAS OFTEN THE CONNECTING LINK

* * *

THESE METHODS ASSIST IN AROUSING A POWERFUL psychic vibration in favour of the earnest student. If he then holds his mind open, and watches for *ideas*, he is on the road to success. The good usually comes to him first in the form of fortunate ideas. These being the direct result of the psychic activity evolved by purposeful act of the student. The idea is thus the connecting link between the psychical and the material and it only remains for the student to develop the opportunities created for him by his thought, or, more exactly, *the opportunities drawn to him by his desire.*

LESSON XIII

THE CONSCIOUS DEVELOPMENT
OF WILL-POWER ∞ THE BASIS OF
WILL-POWER DEVELOPMENT ∞
THE MOST EFFECTIVE METHOD
OF APPLICATION

THE CONSCIOUS DEVELOPMENT
OF WILL-POWER

* * *

IN PRACTISING THE CONSERVATION OF WANTON
mental forces, as described in the earlier lessons, the
Will-Power of the individual is unconsciously developed.
But a conscious development is nevertheless desirable,
as it tends to further increase the self-confidence of
the student and is bound to show itself in his face and
manner even though he may not realise it.

THE BASIS OF WILL-POWER
DEVELOPMENT

* * *

IT IS SUFFICIENT TO SAY THAT THE PURPOSEFUL
accomplishment of any difficult thing, no matter how
unimportant, strengthens the will. Begin with some
trivial thing like trying to draw simultaneously a circle
with one hand and a square with the other, upon a
sheet of paper. Make up your mind to do it just for the
purpose of accomplishing it. When you have at last
succeeded, sit back and absorb the consciousness that

you have conquered something by Will-Power alone. Add this consciousness to your storage battery and proceed to something more practical – perhaps some knotty problem of your domestic life. *Make up your mind to do it*. Use all the consciousness of force you have been storing and don't give it up. Each time you win, you are much stronger than before.

THE MOST EFFECTIVE METHOD OF APPLICATION

* * *

THE MAN OF MOST EFFECTIVE WILL-POWER IS NOT HE who clenches his teeth, hardens his muscles, scowls fiercely and goes at his task in a brutish fashion. He may succeed, but he is wasting energy and cannot compete with the quiet, intelligent, calm and confident man. The latter goes at his task deliberately. He meets failure with a smile and contentedly and patiently goes at it again, *believing* in his own power to succeed. With him this work does not mean a fight, as with the other man, it means merely a period of intelligent activity with only one possible result – Success.

LESSON XIV

Methods of Active Projection.
Lack of Necessity for Same ∞
Relation Between Mental
and Material ∞ A Process of
Induction ∞ Projecting Force
Through Affirmation ∞ Some
Preparation Absolutely Necessary

METHODS OF ACTIVE PROJECTION.
LACK OF NECESSITY FOR SAME

* * *

IN REVIEWING THIS COURSE WHICH I AM NOW ABOUT
to bring to a close some student may say: 'You have
made me understand clearly enough how to be passively
attractive, how to store up this power which draws to
itself, but what I want to know is, *how can I actively
project it?*'

Of course, I could refer him to Lesson XI, but I understand.
He wants something even more immediate and personal.

For all ordinary purposes, it is not necessary to actively
project this force. The fact of its residence and conscious
restraint within you is sufficient to proportionately
attract and accumulate a most gracious offering of
interest, confidence, love and respect from your fellow-
men without an aggressive effort on your part. These
offerings, which in themselves are a rich reward, bring
also in their wake more material favours. They open up
the more conventional and material channels which you
have been vainly trying to open up directly. You failed in
this attempt because you did not realise that the control
of material things *must* be obtained by an intelligent or
harmonious approach through mental channels.

RELATION BETWEEN
MENTAL AND MATERIAL

*   *   *

AS AN ILLUSTRATION LET ME USE THE METAPHOR
of a lake with a beautiful island in the centre of it. The
island represents some material thing you desire –
wealth, for instance. The water of the lake represents
surrounding mental conditions. Your natural desire
is to rush headlong for the island. You find yourself
floundering in the water – mental condition. A
seemingly intangible, but nevertheless an effectual
barrier. To get to the island you must
learn to swim. That is, you must
learn how to master the laws of
mental surroundings before you
can reach material results.

While I cannot sympathise with the
student's impatient desire for an active
projection of his force, when he understands the slower but much surer passive
method, I can cover the point he raises.

*The muscular method, or direct
transmutation of physical into psychic force.*

A Process of Induction

* * *

Adopting the proved electric theory that
to pass a current near another conductor arouses a
sympathetic current in that conductor, let us say you
wish to impress or influence a new acquaintance.
Fix in your mind the fact that he is an instrument
through which mental currents pass; that you are an
instrument which not only generates but receives and
holds fast those currents which you desire.

You may then proceed deliberately to 'draw him out'
conversationally, using the Central Gaze judiciously.
Devote all your tact and skill to do this *unobtrusively*
while at the same time you firmly hold all your own
force and, as it were 'draw yourself in'. By passing
mental currents before him in the form of adroit
questions or suggestions you arouse sympathetic
currents within him, disclosing his likes and dislikes,
and by conversationally stimulating and satisfying
these with a constant undercurrent of subtly expressed
approbation, you soon have him thoroughly in
vibration with you. That is, he likes you and he would
rather be in your society than not. Do not make the
mistake of using cheap flattery. Only the shallowest

are affected by that, but generate in yourself a current of *genuine* kindly interest. You can do this by forcing other interests out of your mind.

With your understanding of the laws of induction and attraction existing between mental currents, you will find that the practice of drawing people to you becomes a fascinating *science*. You will not draw them because you want them particularly, but merely to exercise your power and study the working of the law under varying circumstances.

THERE IS ALWAYS A WAY
OUT OF DIFFICULTIES

There are very few people who do not at times feel
inclined to lose faith in themselves, especially if
things continue to go wrong. Most men in business
experience, at some time in their life, bad business,
when prospects look hopeless. Then is the time that
shows if you are a real man. The man that fights on,
succeeds. It is at just such a time that you need friends
who can show you how to emerge from your difficulty.

If you have no friends equal to the task, you have
enough reserve power to do it yourself. A high bishop
once said: 'No man is a failure until he gives up.' A
brave man is equal to overcome any position. There
have been times that I have found myself in such a
position that there seemed no way out, but I knew
there was a way and, sure enough, a way opened up,
and by experience I have learned that the following
is true: 'That, however hopeless a task may seem, if
you but carry it on, using your faculties to guide you
to safe methods, the way out will appear to you.' This
is an expression meaning that you must go on in
your business career, through all doubts, through all
difficulties, and through all despair.

PROJECTING FORCE
THROUGH AFFIRMATION

* * *

ANOTHER METHOD OF ACTIVE PROJECTION OF influence is through *Affirmation*. For instance, if you are at a social gathering and desire that some certain one present seek an introduction to you of his own accord, the following procedure might be used with variations to suit circumstances. It has been found effective by hundreds of experimenters when conditions are not actually in opposition.

Single out the subject of your experiment. Pass within his range of vision as often as possible without being obtrusive. Use the Central Gaze calmly and pleasantly every time he looks at you. At the same time repeat mentally as if addressing him: 'You want to meet me. You want to meet me.'

Make this a forcible affirmation and seek to send it out to him, as it were, through your eyes.

SOME PREPARATION
ABSOLUTELY NECESSARY

* * *

OF COURSE, NO METHOD EITHER OF ACTIVE OR
of passive attraction is of the slightest value if the
student lets go of his own accumulated force. That is,
if he neglects the constant preservation of force, as
described in the earlier lessons. Further, neither is it
advisable or even reasonably possible to employ any
direct methods such as those just mentioned, until
the student has digested and become proficient in
the general principles of the science outlined in the
foregoing lessons.

A price must be paid on everything, and in the case
of the attainment of Personal Magnetism the price is
the absolute suppression of vanity in any and all its
countless forms.

LESSON XV

CONCLUSION

Conclusion

*　*　*

Just a few words at parting. I have enjoyed writing this Course. I think it is complete and gives you just the information it was meant to give. A word of warning. Beware of bad habits.

Bad habits are among the greatest destroyers of Personal Magnetism. Anyone who is a slave to any bad habit, either mental or physical, may credit the cause of his lack of magnetic personality largely to that fact. Bad habits are a force, and come under the general head of Temptation. They may be dealt with as described in a previous lesson, their force abstracted and stored within you and their evil effects obliterated. And now as a final word of explanation remember this:

You have learned to conserve and project this Force which we call Personal Magnetism. You must never forget that you can make yourself proof at all times by a mere effort of the Will against the mental approach of others who might draw Force from you. You are proof against such draughts when you are positive; self-contained. All through this Course of Lessons I have impressed upon you, without stating the fact in so many words, that you are learning to make a Force that is without individuality or intelligence in itself, a part of your individuality, a part of yourself *by the imposition of your will upon it*. Know, then, finally, that Personal Magnetism is most potent when Force and Will act together in harmony and in unity and become one product.

THE END

HOW TO DEVELOP
PHYSICAL POWER

It is just as important for you to develop your body as
it is to develop your mind. Most men break down just
about the time they begin to know something. If you
want to be magnetic you must keep your body in first-
class shape so that your breath will be sweet, your voice
clear and strong, and a little exertion will not fatigue
you. Make it a rule to devote a little time each day to
physical development. Not once in a while, but each
day. Before going to bed ask yourself these questions:

Have I exercised as I intended?

Have I eaten as I should?

Have I taken the breathing exercises and filled my
lungs with fresh air?

Have I had my bath today?

Did I bathe every part of my body? It matters little
whether you use cold water or not.

Always exercise near an open window. Deep breathing
is the very foundation of good health.

You cannot be magnetic unless you enjoy perfect animal and mental health. If the mind is depressed by grief, tormented by anxiety, or absorbed in sedentary meditations, all the bodily functions become weakened, and Personal Magnetism, so far from being stored to be used to order, leaks from every pore and is wasted. I can't lay too much stress upon the necessity for proper breathing, or the fact that the exercises are useless, except to develop muscle, not magnetism, unless practiced exactly as I say!

The diagrams of the muscular system of the human frame given with this lesson, will show pretty clearly the effects of the various exercises given for developing Personal Magnetism. In the directions for storage of the magnetism, remember the flexing of the body and muscles gives rest, the tensing of the muscles charges them with magnetism, this magnetism courses through the blood, borne along the crimson tide until it is distributed evenly to every part, there to be stored and kept for use, unless wasted by worry, fear, fidgety ways, lack of self-control, or excess in any form.

The first exercise I want you to take is the
American 'dry swim'.

– Stand erect, empty your lungs (exhale) and, holding
your hands to your sides, gradually sink down into the
position of sitting on your heels; then slowly bring your
arms to a horizontal position in front.

– Then slowly inhale, rising easily and gracefully
on tiptoe, throwing the arms back as if
swimming and gradually sinking
back on to your heels as before.

– Repeat this for twenty or
thirty times.

*It is just grand. The
blood tingles and
courses through
the body, and as
the blood courses so
the magnetism flows
through every vein.*

It is one of the most
important exercises, for every
muscle is called into play.

The second exercise is as follows:

– Stand erect, inhale, then, without bending the knee, bend over until your fingers touch the floor, exhale as you rise to an erect position, then, slowly inhaling, bend in similar manner to the left side, exhale as you come up and, inhaling again, slowly bend to the right.

– This must all be done in a deliberate orderly method, taking about fifteen seconds, or twenty even, for each inhalation and exhalation, then, after tensing the muscles for the storage of magnetism, as taught in the last lesson, rest.

You do not require any further physical muscular exercises than these to develop animal magnetism and perfect health, but don't fall into the blunder of thinking you can develop in a week. It will take from two to six months of patient, regular exercise of not less than thirty minutes' daily practice, before you arrive at anything like fitness.

NOTES FROM THE ARCHIVIST

* * *

A PRACTICAL COURSE IN PERSONAL MAGNETISM IS BASED ON material selected from two books, *A Course of Practical Psychic Instruction* from the Psychic Research Company (1901, originally published 1891) and *Concentration and the acquirement of personal magnetism* by O. Hashnu Hara (1906). While being two of the more unheralded titles in the Wellcome Library's collection, these books not only offer insights into lesser-known ideas on wellbeing and mental thought in the 1800s they also point to the growth of a major publishing trend that's with us still in the twenty-first century.

A Course of Practical Psychic Instruction was a five-part work. As well as Personal Magnetism, the work also covered Mind Reading, Hypnotism, ('The Perfect course of instruction in hypnotism, mesmerism, clairvoyance, suggestive therapeutics, and the sleep cure'), Magnetic Healing and Zoism ('a course of instruction in the philosophy and practice of the higher mental science for the attainment of health, happiness and spiritual peace'). Its publisher, the PRC, was based in Chicago and active in the late 1890s and early 1900s. The works published by the PRC were strongly influenced by New Thought, a philosophical and religious movement which emerged in the United States towards the end of the nineteenth century. New Thought emerged in part from the teachings and ideals of Phineas Quimby (1802–66), who promoted the healing qualities of mesmerism. In its attitude to illness, New Thought saw sickness originating in the mind of individuals and therefore encouraged the beneficial and healing effects of 'right thinking'.

This attitude is apparent in *A Course of Practical Psychic Instruction*'s advice on the development and cultivation of Personal Magnetism – note the sections describing the characteristics of the non-magnetic individual: 'he is a grumbler ... he depresses' (p31). On the other hand: 'The successful man is cheerful and hopeful ... you can do your best work only when you are in a cheerful state of mind. When you are out of temper your entire physical machinery is out of working order' (p33).

The notions of Personal Magnetism described in the text have antecedents in the ideas of Animal Magnetism outlined by Franz Mesmer (1734–1815). The ideas of Mesmer, like those of later hypnotists became seen as marginal over the course of the nineteenth century. However, it's worth considering that if we think of hypnosis, mesmerism and 'personal magnetism' as pseudo-science now, we need to acknowledge that other invisible forces such as electricity and magnetism were in themselves seen as mysterious in the 1800s.

While an anonymous work, there is justification for suggesting that the author of *A Course* may have been William Walker Atkinson (1862–1932). An adherent of New Thought – Atkinson had come to the movement after working as a lawyer and suffering a breakdown – he professed his beliefs as author of multiple works (estimates have suggested over 100 books) under multiple aliases: Theron Q. Dumont, Yogi Ramacharaka, Swami Bhakta Vishita and, it's been suggested, O Hashnu Haru.

Such aliases as these point to the increasing interest in Eastern thought – particularly that associated with the Indian sub-continent – by the end of the nineteenth century. The co-founder of the Theosophical Society – a near cousin in many ways to the New Thought movement – Helena Blavatsky, claimed that encounters with mysterious spiritual masters in Tibet radically altered her spiritual awareness. Very much rooted in the swirl of spiritual movements at the end of the nineteenth century and the beginning of the twentieth, these works should perhaps be read with an eye towards works similarly aimed at self-transformation and the power of positive thought, which were to gain traction in the forthcoming decades.

Consider lines such as 'the more prosperous you look the more success you will attract' (p25) and 'You should form the habit of looking ahead: of planning what you want to accomplish. You may think this all nonsense, but it works out, and all you want is results' (p48). Such quotes would not look out of place in best-selling works such as Dale Carengie's *How to Win Friends and Influence People* (1936) or Norman Vincent Peale's *The Power of Positive Thinking* (1952). And what better way to influence people and think positively than if you have a magnetic personality?

We may smile at its contents now, but in many ways *A Course of Practical Psychic Instruction* points out a road to travel which the self-help gurus still follow.

Ross MacFarlane
Wellcome Library